THE SPIRITUAL JOURNEY

by Mark Conner

Understanding the Stages of Faith

Copyright © 2018 Mark Conner
Amazon paperback Edition

All rights reserved. This book or any portion thereof may not be reproduced or used in any manner whatsoever without the express written permission of the publisher except for the use of brief quotations in a book review.

Published by Conner Ministries Inc

Email: mark.conner7@icloud.com
WEB: www.markconner.com.au
BLOG: www.blog.markconner.com.au

Unless otherwise indicated, all quotations from the Bible are from the *Holy Bible: New International Version*®. NIV®. Copyright ©1973, 1978, 1984 by International Bible Society. Used by permission of Zondervan. All rights reserved.

Scriptures marked NLT are taken from the *Holy Bible, New Living Translation*. Copyright ©1996, 2004, 2007 by Tyndale House Foundation. Used by permission of Tyndale House Publishers, Inc., Carol Stream, Illinois 60188. All rights reserved. Used by permission.

Scriptures marked TMB are taken from *The Message*. Copyright © 1993, 1994, 1995, 1996, 2000, 2001, 2002. Used by permission of NavPress Publishing Group.

Front cover designed at www.canva.com

WHY I WROTE THIS BOOK

1. To help the average person recognize God's presence and activity in their daily life.
2. To provide a roadmap for the journey of faith so people can better understand God's work in their life.
3. To help those further along in their faith to go deeper and be better guides for other people in their spiritual journey.
4. To help church leaders embrace a more holistic view of life of faith and to provide them with a framework or model for teaching people about the common contours of the spiritual journey.

WHY YOU SHOULD READ THIS BOOK

1. If you are interested in knowing God personally or experiencing him more in your life.
2. If you would like to gain a greater understanding of where God has been at work in your life and where he could be working now.
3. If you would benefit from having a map for how the journey of faith often unfolds for people.
4. If you would like to be a helpful guide to other people in their spiritual journey.
5. If you are a teacher, speaker, coach, or spiritual director to people in the area of their spirituality and desire to improve your helping skills.

ENDORSEMENTS

"Christians throughout the world are asking themselves what lifelong discipleship really means in today's fast-changing culture. Mark Conner has written a thoughtful guide, combining his own personal experience with insightful biblical and theological reflection – all of it offering practical ways to live as faithful followers of Jesus."

John Drane
UK Theologian and Best-Selling Author

"If you want to move out of safety zones and follow Jesus' trail of the full human being through the seasons of life, this book gives some great tips born of the author's experience."

Ray Simpson
Best selling author of *Celtic Christianity* and Founding Guardian of the International Community of Aidan and Hilda in Lindisfarne, UK

"Too often in our very individualistic culture, we assume what we are going through in our faith journey is unique. Mark Conner's book 'The Spiritual Journey' helps us understand that we are not alone in our various stages of faith. With insight, clarity, helpful descriptions and personal stories, Mark has produced a book that should be compulsory reading for Christians of all ages."

Cheryl McCallum
Minister, Church Leader, experienced Theological Educator

"When you read the Hebrew Scriptures you discover a people growing in their journey of faith and understanding of God. It helps to reflect on Israel's progressive redemptive story in light of our own faith pilgrimage. Mark's book provides insight, stories and excellent application to assist us as we contemplate our progression with a God who loves us through all our stages of faith."

Nicole Conner
Writer, Blogger and Storyteller

"Mark's teaching on navigating the spiritual journey is unique, biblical and helpful for everyone wanting to become a fully devoted follower of Jesus. Our leadership team, made up of all ages and stages of faith, were blessed by Mark's insights and discovered new ways to draw closer to God and become more like Jesus in their season of life and ministry".

Jason Elsmore
Senior Pastor, Gateway Baptist Church, Brisbane Australia

"Following Jesus is a lifelong quest – a journey. In this book Mark Conner gives clarity and insight to the stages we can expect to pass through on that journey. Full of biblical wisdom and inspiring personal reflections, this is a book for everyone on the journey, no matter what age or stage."

David Ratten
Churches of Christ Minister, Experienced Church Leader, Speaker and Mentor

"The Bible compares our life to 'a mist that appears for a little time'. However, the inner world of a person is as complicated as a universe. Passing through different periods of development, we are faced with challenges and difficult circumstances. This book by Mark Conner gives answers to many crucial questions and helps everyone on this unique journey."

Vasily Dotsenko
Senior Pastor of Cornerstone Church, Novosibirsk, Russia

TABLE OF CONTENTS

Metaphors for Life	9
Awareness	15
Growth	25
Contribution	31
The Wall	39
Surrender	49
Paradox	55
Love	59
Putting It All Together	67
Recommended Resources	71
About Mark Conner	73

METAPHORS FOR LIFE

Life is beautiful. It really is. It is full of wonder, surprises, excitement, and mystery. Yet, for the vast majority of people, it also includes in a good dose of pain, disappointment, and unexpected twists along the way.

We arrive into this world with no instruction manual or map. No tool box or nap sack. Only bright hope for the future, if only in our parents eyes. From our first breath we move forward, awkwardly at first then gradually with more steadiness and purpose.

How are we to understand this gift called life? There are many metaphors, pictures, and images to help us view its essence. Here are a few of them.

A Story

If your life were viewed as a story with many chapters, what genre would it be? Is your life a drama, a comedy, an adventure, a suspense film, an action story, a romance, or a horror show? Maybe an epic narrative is the best description.

Whatever your story has been so far, you are the author of your own story. Life is not so much what has happened to us as it is how we re-tell the narrative to ourselves and to others. Where have you come from? Who are you now, as the main character in your story? Where are you going? What could the next episode in your story be?

Seasons

The physical seasons can be symbolic of the seasons of our soul or the seasons of our life. We will all experience the chill of winter, the joy of spring, the abundance of summer, and the loss of autumn (or fall as they say in America) somewhere in our life, most likely multiple times. Life brings us a continual series of endings and beginnings, with the transitions or liminal spaces between them. Grief and joy both come along for the ride.

What seasons have you been through over the last few years? What did they feel like? What season is it for you right now? What does the atmosphere and environment feel like? What's in the air? What's up ahead or around the corner for you?

Age Stages

Time is the one constant in life. It is always moving and we become a little bit older each and every day. As we do, we gradually move through the stages of childhood, adolescence, young adulthood, middle age, and eventually old age. Yes, the arrow of time is continually moving forward and it seems to speed up as we become older.

What stages of life have you navigated so far? What were they like? What is your current stage of life? How would you describe it? What's your next age stage? Who could you learn from who has already been where you are going?

A Race

The image of a race provides a vivid picture of our lives. There is a beginning, forward movement, obstacles along the way, and a finish line somewhere over the horizon. How is your race going?

Maybe you are going strong, running well and with full gusto and energy. Or maybe you are slowing down because of fatigue, a loss of passion, or uncertainty due to a change in terrain or even an upcoming intersection. Maybe you have stopped, because of tragedy, a stumble along the way, or simply because you are feeling discouraged. Or could it be that you have detoured and lost your way?

Wherever you are in your race (and I have been in all of these conditions) be encouraged that it's never too late to get back on track, to get going again, and to renew your passion for life. Winning is not about never falling down but about rising each time you do. Make a choice to never quit and to do your best to finish well.

The Day of Your Life

Moses in his wisdom once wrote:

> "Our days may come to seventy years, or eighty, if our strength endures ... they quickly pass, and we fly away ... Teach us to number our days, that we may gain a heart of wisdom." Psalm 90:10-12.

Yes, time is moving and so is your life. It is a sobering fact. What would it look like to view your life as a single day from 6.00 am through to midnight?

If you lived to 80 years of age (the average man lives a little less and the average woman lives a little longer today), what time is it for you?

- At 15 - It's 9.22 a.m. It's time to get up and at it!
- At 20 - It's 10.30 a.m. The day is well under way.
- At 30 - It's 12.45 p.m. You are already into the afternoon of your life.
- At 40 - It's 3.00 p.m.
- At 50 - It's 5.15 p.m. The sun is almost about to set! Of course, in Australia, and a number of other countries, we have daylight saving time so you have a little longer before the sun sets in the summer!
- At 60 - It's 7.30 p.m. The evening hours are beginning.
- At 70 - It's 9.45 p.m. It is getting late.
- At 80 - It's midnight!
- 80+ - You are into 'time on'!

Hopefully, that was not too depressing for you. The truth is that many of us will live much longer. My dad is currently 91 years of age and one of his life-long friends recently turned 101! But the reality is that the day of our life is moving and nothing can stop it. That fact alone should motivate us to make the best of this one life we have.

A Journey

Another way to view our life is through that of a journey. A journey has stages, involves movement, actions, change, progress, stops, detours, hills and valleys, as well as surprises.

Ancient Israel underwent a journey - out of Egypt (the Exodus), through the wilderness, with all its wanderings, and eventually into the promised land. Their journey becomes a metaphor for the life of faith. Personal and spiritual growth occur over a period of time and always involves a process that is very much like a journey. This is the metaphor that this book is built around.

I am particularly grateful for the insights I have gleaned from *The Critical Journey: Stages in the Life of Faith* by Janet O. Hagberg and Robert A. Guelich. Their writing has shaped many of the ideas and concepts I will share with you in this book. I have simply used some different names for the common stages of faith and re-ordered a few of them, as well as connected them to my own experience of the spiritual journey.

Hagberg and Guelich note that the idea of movement through stages or phases within the life of faith has a long history in the Church. Several early leaders spoke of journeys, both inward and outward. These include people such as Augustine, John of the Cross, Francis of Assisi, and Ignatius Loyola. More recently, various models have been proposed by a variety of thinkers and authors (see the recommended resources on page 71).

When you are on a journey, it helps to have a **map** of the terrain and a **guide** to help you along the way. I'll be presenting such a map to you and I'll endeavor to be a guide to help you with what I've learned and what I have experienced in my own journey, as imperfect as it has been.

This particular map of **the stages of faith** is more *descriptive* than it is *prescriptive*. In other words, I'll describe what *often* happens, not what must or *should* happen. Also, our spiritual journey is rarely linear or in a straight line. There are many curves, twists, and surprises along the way. Sometimes we seem to move in circles or in random patterns that don't make sense at the time. Welcome to your life. Welcome to the spiritual journey. Let's begin .

AWARENESS

Everyone begins their spiritual journey with an **awareness** of God. Here is where we discover, accept, and/or recognize the presence and reality of God. Someone bigger than us exists and is reaching out to us. This experience may occur in childhood or later in life as adults.

For some people this is a very identifiable experience. It occurs at a specific moment in time when everything suddenly changes. For others, there is more of a gradual realization of God with no certainty as to where or when the awareness took place. Either way, we simply become *aware* that God is there.

Waking Up

These experiences are often referred to as 'conversion stories'. In many ways, they are comparable to waking up from sleep. Some people have what could be called an 'alarm clock conversion'. Suddenly, they are awake!

Saul was on the road to Damascus to persecute more Christians when he encountered Jesus (see Acts 9). In a moment, his life was transformed and the direction of his life radically changed. For other people, their experience of waking up is more gradual in that they simply find themselves awake with no memory of exactly when or even how it occurred.

A sense of awe is sometimes the major contributing factor to a conversion experience, whether that be through the beauty of creation, the joy of an answered prayer, the wonder of a new born baby, or some kind of miraculous experience. For others, a sense of need leads them towards God. When we are at the bottom or in a desperate situation we often look up and reach out to see if God is there. We are often most open to God in our pain ,more so than when everything is going smoothly.

Other people look to God as an answer to their quest for meaning and purpose in life. For others, it is during times of transition that they find faith. In my own country of Australia, it is interesting to observe how many immigrants are coming to faith in the churches. When the routine of people's lives and environments are disrupted they are often more open to change and to new experiences.

This 'waking up' experience may happen while we are alone or when we are with other people. It may happen informally or in a more formal environment, such as a church meeting. Each person's journey is unique, as is their coming to an awareness of God in their life.

My Story

I grew up in a Christian family. I am a 'PK' - a 'Preacher's Kid' or a 'TO', as my dad used to refer to me as - a 'Theological Offspring'. Our family attended church three times every Sunday - mornings at our local church, afternoon for a combined meeting with other related congregations, and evenings back at our local church. Then there were Wednesday night Bible studies and Friday night kid's club or youth group meetings.

When I was eight years of age, our family visited America where we spent 18 months traveling up and down the West Coast while my dad spoke at numerous church camps and Bible conferences. I would always try out the kid's program but inevitably I eventually became bored so I would come and sit on the front row in the big people's meetings where my dad was speaking. I began taking notes to help pass the time. 'End times' were often the topic of the day back then in the 1970s and I remember asking my dad before one meeting, "Are you going to speak on the Antichrist today, dad, or aren't these people ready for that?" Welcome to my world.

Apparently, I made a commitment to become a Christian somewhere in those early years although I don't remember when or how. Nevertheless, my whole world was one in which God was talked about and known, at least by all the people around me.

In my late teens, I decided I wanted to know God for myself. I decided to take a 3 day fast. My family lived in Portland, Oregon at the time, in a typical American home composed of a basement, a ground floor, an upstairs, and an attic. I headed for the attic with my Bible, an empty notebook and a pen. I was going to meet with God.

The first day went by. Nothing happened, except I was a little hungry. The second day went by much more slowly. Again, nothing happened. Now I was really hungry. The third day came and I was starving. "God, where are you?", I thought. "I'm here! Why aren't you?" There had been no audible voice, no angel showing up, and no scroll dropping down from heaven. I had done my part. Why hadn't God done his? I was starting to feel disappointed, with a mild sense of frustration and even doubt beginning to grow inside my heart.

Late in the afternoon, I flipped through my Bible one more time and happened to land on 1 Samuel chapter 3. There I read the story of a boy named Samuel. I was captured by what unfolded. God called to him but he did not yet recognize God's voice so he went and asked the priest, Eli, if he had called. No, he hadn't. Again it happened. Same result. The third time, the old priest finally realized that God was trying to speak to the young boy Samuel. He told him to go lay down again and next time to say, "Speak, Lord, your servant is listening."

Samuel did so and this time he recognized God's voice for the first time. So began a close and intimate relationship between God and this young prophet-in-the-making. It all made sense. After all, if you never have a conversation with someone, how can you ever know them or genuinely speak on their behalf?

As I finished reading the story, a flood of thoughts suddenly flowed into my mind, quietly but ever so clearly. "Mark, I am speaking to you all the time. You just haven't yet learned to recognize my voice. Often you miss it because you are looking for the spectacular and in doing so you don't see me in the natural and the everyday. I am speaking to you through the Bible when you open its pages, through your parents, through the preacher in church on Sunday, through the circumstances of your life, and through the gentle promptings of my Holy Spirit who lives within you." I wrote all of this in my notebook as quickly as it came to me. I was suddenly *aware* of God speaking directly to me - for the first time. I was overcome with a sense of warmth and peace. It was a holy moment yet it felt so 'normal'. My life has never been the same since.

Later on I was to realize that when God speaks to us, his voice speaks through the medium of our mind, which also has a voice. All thoughts flow through our mind, regardless of their source and therefore they often sound the same to us. For example, Peter had thoughts of revelation directly from God the Father flow into his mind about who Jesus was (Matthew 16:13-20) then immediately after this he had thoughts planted there by Satan himself (Matthew 16:21-23). Not long after this, he blurted out his own thoughts about building a few shelters on the mountain where Jesus was being transfigured only to be told in no uncertain terms to be quiet for a moment (Matthew 17:1-5).

In the same way, the challenge for us is to learn to discern the source of our thoughts - whether they are coming from ourselves, from the enemy, or from God. Often we mix them up but we can grow in our awareness of when God is speaking to us The enemy's thoughts are usually negative and full of doubt and condemnation while God's thoughts are full of faith and are characterized by love, peace, and joy.

Your Story?

Enough about me. What about you? Have you become aware of God? If so, what happened? When and how did it occur? What was your life like before, during, and after this experience?

Or maybe, like me when I was a teenager, you are keen to know God for yourself but he hasn't shown up yet. The good news is that if we seek him, we will find him. Even better news is that he is pursuing us with his relentless love. His desire is that every human being know him personally and therefore we know that he is making efforts for that to become a reality. God doesn't want anyone to perish (to live without him) but to have 'eternal life', which can be defined as knowing God personally (see 2 Peter 3:9 and John 17:3).

Once we become aware of God for ourselves, we can join him in helping others become aware of him. God is a God of mission and he calls us to simply join him in his work right where we are. Sometimes you hear people talk about those people who are "far from God" but this is not based on truth or reality. Listen to what the apostle Paul said in a message he gave in the marketplace in the pagan city of Athens, which was full of philosophers and truth-seekers:

*"God did this so that they would seek him and perhaps reach out for him and find him, though **he is not far from***

any one of us. *'For in him we live and move and have our being.'" Acts 17:27-28.*

God is **not far** from every person on earth. That's really good news! He is close to them. They just don't realize it yet. Hopefully, soon they will wake up and become aware of God and his love for them.

God's Presence

The truth is that we don't lack the presence of God. God is omni-present. He is everywhere at once. There is no where we can go where he is not already there. Take the time to read the lyrics of a song that King David wrote many centuries ago (Psalm 139:1-18):

"You have searched me, Lord, and you know me. You know when I sit and when I rise; you perceive my thoughts from afar. You discern my going out and my lying down; you are familiar with all my ways. Before a word is on my tongue you, Lord, know it completely. You hem me in behind and before, and you lay your hand upon me. Such knowledge is too wonderful for me, too lofty for me to attain.

Where can I go from your Spirit? Where can I flee from your presence? If I go up to the heavens, you are there; if I make my bed in the depths, you are there. If I rise on the wings of the dawn, if I settle on the far side of the sea, even there your hand will guide me, your right hand will hold me fast. If I say, 'Surely the darkness will hide me and the light become night around me,' even the darkness will not be dark to you; the night will shine like the day, for darkness is as light to you.

For you created my inmost being; you knit me together in my mother's womb. I praise you because I am fearfully and wonderfully made; your works are wonderful, I know that full well. My frame was not hidden from you when I was made in the secret place, when I was woven together in the depths of the earth. Your eyes saw my unformed body; all the days ordained for me were written in your book before one of them came to be.

How precious to me are your thoughts, God! How vast is the sum of them! Were I to count them, they would outnumber the grains of sand –when I awake, I am still with you."

Yes, God *is* all around you now. He is with you and he is for you. We don't have to ask for his presence. One of Jesus' names is Immanuel, which literally means "God with us". His last recorded words to his followers were, "Yes, I am with you always, to the very end of the age" (Matthew 28:20). **We don't lack God's presence. We simply lack awareness.**

There is an intriguing story about Abraham's grandson, Jacob, recorded for us in Genesis 28:10-22. Jacob is traveling out in the rugged Judean desert in a 'certain place' between Beersheba and Harran that doesn't even have a name. He goes to sleep and has a spectacular dream of a stairway between heaven and earth with angels ascending and descending on it. God then speaks to him in the dream, making some huge promises to him about his future. After this, Jacob wakes up and declares:

> "Surely the Lord was in this place and I was **not aware** of it (Genesis 28:16)."

He then said:

> "How awesome is this place! This is none other than the house of God; this is the gate of heaven (Genesis 28:17)."

What turns an ordinary place into an awesome place? One thing - an awareness of God. Jacob woke up to the reality of God's presence … right where he was. May we do the same. This is the beginning, the first stage, of our spiritual journey.

For Further Reading

4 Keys to Hearing God's Voice by Mark Virkler (Destiny Image, Shippensburg, PA. 2010).

Celtic Christianity: Deep Roots for a Modern Faith by Ray Simpson (Anamchara Books, Vestal, NY. 2016).

Everything Belongs: The Gift of Contemplative Prayer by Richard Rohr (The Crossroad Publishing Company, New York, NY. 2003).

God Was In This Place and I Did Not Know It by Rabbi Lawrence Kushner (Jewish Lights, Woodstock, VM. 1993).

Mere Christianity by C.S. Lewis (Harper Publishing, San Francisco, CA. 2009).

Prayer: The Mightiest Force in the World by Frank Charles Laubach (Martino Fine Books, Eastford, CT. 2012).

The Practice of the Presence of God by Brother Lawrence (Martino Fine Books, Eastford, CT. 2016).

The Present Perfect: Finding God in the Now by Gregory A Boyd (Zondervan, Grand Rapids, MI. 2010).

The Ragamuffin Gospel: Good News for the Bedraggled, Beat-Up and Burnout by Brennan Manning (Multnomah, Portland, OR. 2005).

The Reason for God by Tim Keller (Viking, New York, NY. 2008).

What's So Amazing About Grace? by Phillip Yancey (Zondervan, Grand Rapids, MI. 2002).

GROWTH

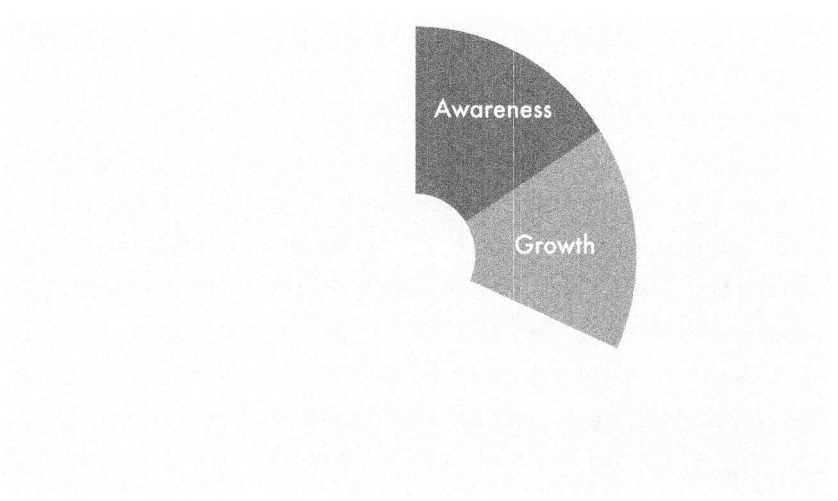

Now that we are aware of God we usually enter a stage of **growth** in our faith. We want to do more than believe in God. We start to follow him and seek to please him with our lives. Disciples see Jesus as the leader of their life.

The Community of Faith

Usually, by this stage we have discovered other people who have also become aware of God and this group, whether large or small, formal or informal, becomes an important part of our faith journey.

Part of our learning about God is through others who know him also and have been walking with him longer than we have. This is especially true in the early days of our faith journey as we are much like apprentices and novices who are somewhat unsure and even insecure in our newfound relationship with God.

The community of faith, most often in some form or expression of 'church', becomes like a family to us. It is here that we experience a sense of belonging, identity, and security. We are loved and accepted, much like children learning to walk this spiritual journey.

However, when we are surrounded by this support system but don't have a genuine personal awareness of God for ourselves it can lead to what is referred to as a 'socialized faith'. This is a mere imitation of real faith. We simply become a product of our environment without having a personal sense of God in our own life apart from the group we are a part of. This can particularly happen to young people who grow up in Christian homes or in the church but who never encounter God personally. Faith can so easily degenerate into merely a set of religious beliefs, spiritual rituals, or a long list of do's and don't's, rather than a personal and genuine relationship with God.

Spiritual Growth

Spiritual growth is a *process* that takes time. It is not instant. It is a journey. It is also a *partnership* between God and us. There are things we do and there are things that God alone can do. Notice this interdependence in Paul's following statement in Philippians 2:12-13:

> *"Therefore, my dear friends, as you have always obeyed— not only in my presence, but now much more in my absence – continue to **work out** your salvation with fear and trembling, for it is God who **works in** you to will and to act in order to fulfill his good purpose."*

When driving a **motorboat**, you are in control and can steer the vessel wherever you want it to go across the water. However, in a **sailboat**, there are things that you can do, such as place the vessel on the water and hoist the sails, but if the wind is not blowing, you aren't going anywhere. Spiritual growth is very much like this. There are things we can do to position ourselves for transformation but all change is by the Spirit of God at work in our lives, not through our own self-effort.

God works as we work. Without our work, we may grow old but we will never grow up. Maturity requires the acceptance of responsibility and an ongoing commitment to the process of change in our lives.

Spiritual Disciplines

Spiritual growth is also more about **training** than **trying**. We cannot change or become like Jesus simply through trying hard. It is not possible. Listen to Paul again in 1 Timothy 4:7-8:

> *"Have nothing to do with godless myths and old wives' tales; rather,* **train yourself to be godly**. *For physical training is of some value, but godliness has value for all things, holding promise for both the present life and the life to come."*

Paul does not say to his young prodigy, Timothy, "*Try* to be like Jesus". He says, "*Train* yourself to be godly." The Greek word translated "train" in our English Bibles is the word *gymnazo*, from which we get the English word 'gymnastics'. Paul is urging Timothy to engage in a life of exercises and disciplines that will, as Dallas Willard says, "Enable you to do what you cannot do by will power alone."

We cannot run a marathon, play a musical instrument, or speak a new language simply by trying. But if we will enter a life of training and commit ourselves to exercises and disciplines, we can train ourselves to do activities such as these that mere trying will never accomplish. It is the same with spiritual growth in the life of faith.

There are many spiritual practices, disciplines, or habits of transformation that we can engage in. **Disciplines of engagement** include celebration, prayer, reading the Scriptures, fellowship with others, and serving with our gifts. **Disciplines of disengagement** include sacrifice, doing good deeds in secret rather than to be seen, fasting, silence, and solitude.

Spiritual disciplines aren't necessarily hard, In fact, they become self-reinforcing as we see the benefit of them in our life. They are also not a means to earn favor with God. We don't 'work for' our salvation. We 'work out' our salvation. It is a response to God's love for us not something we do in order to earn God's love.

Most importantly, spiritual disciplines are not a barometer of our spirituality. The key issue is not the number or length of the exercises we are doing but whether or not we are becoming more like Jesus. They are a means to an end and that end is spiritual growth.

My Story

My personal growth has greatly been enhanced by other people of faith and the various church communities I have belonged to over the years. I have had many mentors, teachers, examples, and models to follow. Without them, I would not be who I am today nor would I be where I am on my own spiritual journey. We need one another. Fellowship is a faith and character-shaping activity.

I have also benefited greatly by a variety of spiritual exercises that I have engaged in personally over the years, including prayer, times of solitude, and fasting. Bible reading has also played a big part in my own growth and faith development.

For example, when I was a teenager, our youth pastor encouraged us to read a proverb for every day of the month. I did this for many years and gained much wisdom from it. I also had a few times when God grabbed my attention in quite profound ways.

One time I was hanging around the wrong crowd at school and had begun helping a friend to steal items from the local K-Mart store. We were into bikes in those days and he stole various parts and extra goodies. This was before the days of security cameras. I would help him by watching that the aisle was clear or opening the packet but I justified my involvement because I didn't do the actual stealing. He did.

I was still attending church and occasionally reading my Bible. One morning, I came upon a proverb in my little Living Bible that said, "He who is a partner to a thief is a fool!" Wow, did God have my attention. I promptly called my friend and said I was out. Who knows where I might have ended up if I hadn't had that transforming moment with God and my Bible.

Your Story?

What about you? What has contributed to your growth in your spiritual journey so far? What part have other people played? What spiritual experiences have been influential, such as water baptism, baptism in the Holy Spirit, or partaking of the Lord's supper? What spiritual disciplines have been helpful to you? Are your trying or training to be like Jesus? What could you do to further enhance your own growth as a person of faith and in your own relationship with God? In what area would you like to grow the most and what practical steps could you take towards that now?

Take some time to think about your answers to those important questions before moving on to read about the next stage of faith. To dig deeper on this subject of growth, check out the following resources.

For Further Reading

Deepening Your Conversation With God by Ben Paterson (Bethany House Publishers, Minneapolis, MN. 2001).

How People Grow by Henry Cloud and John Townsend (Harper Collins Publishing, New York, NY. 2009).

Finding Our Way Again: The Return to the Ancient Practices by Brian McClaren (Thomas Nelson, Nashville, TN. 2010).

The Celebration of Discipline by Richard Foster (Hodder & Stoughton, London, UK. 2012).

The Spirit of the Disciplines by Dallas Willard (HarperOne Publishers, San Francisco, CA. 2009).

The Life You've Always Wanted: Spiritual Disciplines for Ordinary People by John Ortberg (Zondervan, Grand Rapids, MI. 2015).

CONTRIBUTION

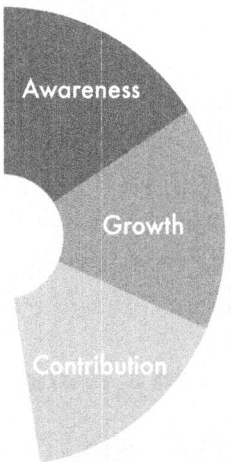

Every human being has a need for **contribution** and this is often the next stage of our spiritual journey. We have this inbuilt desire to be useful with our lives. I have never met anyone who wanted to be useless!

This stage begins with an exploration of what our unique contribution might be. We want to give back for all that God has done for us. We start to discover, develop, and deploy our gifts for the benefit of others. We begin to DO something about our faith. This may be in the form of volunteering for a particular ministry, activity or cause. Eventually, it may even include taking on extra responsibility such as leadership.

We gradually realize that we are not just saved to go to heaven when we die but that we have a calling right here, right now to God's church and God's cause on the earth. Over time we start to develop confidence in who we are and we see our value to the community and our world. This can be very fulfilling and rewarding.

Our contribution also helps us grow and it strengthens our own faith. Our relationship with God is enhanced as we learn to depend on him more. We feel his presence and his power at times in tangible ways as we serve. This stage can be quite exciting as we see the fruit and results of our efforts. It's a time of activity, action, and productivity. We also often start to receive recognition, respect, and praise from others as our influence and impact grows.

Your Work, God's Work

God is a worker. Father, Son and Holy Spirit partnered together to bring about the creation of our universe. God rejoiced in his work then rested on the seventh day (Genesis 2:2). Right now, God is busy with the work of redemption, getting the world back on track after the detour caused by the first human's failure to obey his commands.

We were created to work too. Adam was placed in a garden to tend it (Genesis 2:15) and then he was given the project of naming all of the animals (Genesis 2:19). Work adds meaning to our lives and provides the means for us to earn income to meet our needs and those of others. God gives us the ability to earn wealth (Deuteronomy 8:17-18). Note that God is in the power-giving business not the money-giving business.

The majority of people in the biblical story had jobs and careers outside of the temple activities, where the priests and Levites had their work to do.

- **Abraham** was a herder of vast flocks of sheep, goats, donkeys, cattle, and perhaps even camels. Many modern scholars think he was also a trader, managing donkey caravans and doing business from Turkey to Egypt.
- **Deborah** was a judge in Israel.
- **David** was a king, responsible for an entire nation.
- **Nehemiah** was an employee in the king's palace.
- **Daniel** was a government official.
- **Amos** was a farmer.
- **Jesus** was a carpenter up until the age of 30. He had to deal with customers, products, suppliers and orders.
- **Paul** was a tentmaker, or more likely a leather-worker, who funded his church work through the profits he made (sometimes in partnership with Aquila and Priscilla).
- **Peter**, **James** and **John** were fishermen who had a fishing business with their father.

Your daily work is part of your life contribution. In fact, your contribution includes every area of your life - serving your family, your friends, your church community, your school your workplace, your neighborhood, your local community and your world. Don't buy into the dualism that sees only church life as 'sacred' and everything else as 'secular'. All of life is sacred. Listen to what the apostle Paul says about this in Colossians 3:17:

"Whatever you do, whether in word or deed, do it all in the name of the Lord Jesus, giving thanks to God the Father through him."

'Whatever' is a big, all-encompassing word! It means and includes *everything* we do in our daily lives. Whatever you do, do it in the name of, or representing, Jesus Christ. That's quite a contribution.

Your Unique SHAPE

American pastor, Rick Warren, is the master of acronyms. He came up with the concept of each person having a unique SHAPE. Our **SHAPE** includes our **S**piritual gifts (every Christian has one or more), our **H**eart (or what we are passionate about), our **A**bilities (including our natural talents), our unique **P**ersonality, and our life **E**xperience. Nothing is wasted and God uses everything in our lives to SHAPE us for effective service.

My Story

When I was young, I wasn't sure what I wanted to be when I grew up. As a result, I dabbled in a variety of interests, hobbies and part-time jobs throughout my schooling years. I worked in a cabinet making shop (sweeping wood shavings from the floor), in a book bindery, for a builder's renovator, and as a printer.

Because of my love for music, I started volunteering for the music ministry in our church - playing the piano, singing and leading worship, first at youth group then in big church. Eventually, I was asked to lead this ministry and I did so as a volunteer for five years. Then I accepted an offer of a staff role as Music Director. I loved it. In those days, I thought that worship was the most important ministry in the church. The best meetings were when no one preached. We just worshipped God. I thought I would do this the rest of my life.

Then, a few years later, my wife and I were asked to lead the youth ministry. We were hesitant at first, as we were newly married but we decided to give it a go anyway. I had to come out from behind the piano, learn to speak and work with young people. Over time, we really enjoyed it and then I realized that youth ministry was the most important ministry in the church!

We thought we would be in youth ministry for the rest of our lives, but after five years I was asked to be the church's Administrator. I said, "What's that?" Well, I took the offer, completed a Diploma of Business Management degree and grew to love this role. Then I realized that being organized is the most important thing in the church.

As you can imagine, about this time I was having an identity crisis. I thought, "Who am I - a worship leader, a youth pastor or a church administrator?" You see, we often find our identity in what we do rather than who we are. I had to realize that my value and identity was in the fact that I was a child of God and that my serving roles may change over time. I should do what I am doing now with the commitment that I would do it for the rest of my life but at the same time holding it lightly enough that I am willing to lay it down at a moment's notice. This was all part of me growing up in my faith.

I also came to realize that God's will often makes sense looking back, not when we are in a particular time or situation. Eventually, I became an Associate Minister and then after ten years in a variety of ministry staff roles I became the Senior Minister of our church, a role I held for the next twenty-two years. The experience I gained through the various ministries I was involved in along the way proved invaluable to this responsibility. Again, nothing is wasted in God.

All that to say, my contribution over the years has played a huge part in my journey of faith. Although I have served and given much of my time, energy and resources, I have grown so much myself. I have become a better person, developed many character qualities, made good friends, learned more about God, seen God at work in amazing ways, and deepened my faith - all because of contribution.

Your Story

What about you? What has been your contribution along your spiritual journey? How do your see your job, career or vocation fitting into this? Do you know your SHAPE? What energizes you the most? What causes are you passionate about? What are you good at? What are you *not* good at? What drains you? What makes you angry? How has contribution affected your faith and relationship with God? Have you changed your contribution over the years? What would you like to do next? If you could do anything with your life, what would it be?

Why not take some time to think about these questions before moving on to explore the next stage of faith. Answering them can help you gain further understanding about the unique contribution you are called to make in the world. So can the following excellent resources.

For Further Reading

Every Good Endeavor: Connecting Your Work to God's Plan for the World by Tim Keller (Hodder and Stoughton, London, UK. 2012).

God at Work: Live Each Day with Purpose by Ken Costa (Thomas Nelson, Nashville, TN. 2016).

Money Talks: Practical Principles for Becoming Financially Free by Mark Conner (Conner Ministries, Melbourne, Australia. 2018).

Discover Your Spiritual Gifts the Network Way by Bruce L. Bugbee (Zondervan, Grand Rapids, MI. 2005).

The Purpose Driven Church: Growth Without Compromising Your Message and Mission by Rick Warren (Zondervan, Grand Rapids, MI. 2010).

The Purpose Driven Life: What on Earth Am I Here For? by Rick Warren (Zondervan, Grand Rapids, MI. 2012).

What Color is Your Parachute? The Job Hunter's Workbook (Fourth Edition) by Richard N. Bolles (Ten Speed Press, Emeryville, CA. 2012).

Your Spiritual Gifts Can Help Your Church Grow by Peter Wagner (Gospel Light, Ventura, CA. 1994).

THE WALL

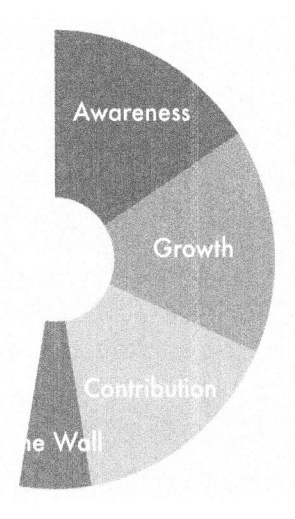

I wish we could stop here and say, "That's it! Come to Jesus, grow as a Christian, and use your gifts and Jesus will be back soon." But there is more, much more to the spiritual journey. To go deeper in our faith means that there will be some bumps along the way, some challenges and maybe even a crisis here or there.

This next stage of our spiritual journey is when we hit **the Wall**, as it were. It is accompanied by the emergence of questions, doubts and uncertainty. Our faith isn't working quite like it did earlier on. This stage is often caused by a life challenge, a crisis, or a faith test. We suddenly feel very vulnerable. This is a hugely unsettling time in our lives.

My Story

My first experience of the Wall was when I was sixteen years of age. I have an older sister who by then was married and had left home, so I was the only child now living with my parents. We had a young Bible College student by the name of Robert come and board with us. He was twenty years of age and he became like an older brother to me.

One summer break, my parents and I went away for some holidays. Robert stayed home as he had work to do. I still remember the moment we returned. My dad was unlocking the front door of our house and the telephone was ringing. He ran to answer it, as we brought our things inside the house. We saw that my dad was visibly shaken by the conversation with the person on the other end of the phone. It was one of Robert's best friends. He had called to tell us that Robert had tragically drowned. He was swimming in a river with some other young adults and accidentally got caught under the water by some tree branches. Despite a friend's desperate attempts to save him, he was gone.

His family and all of us were devastated. How could this have happened? Robert was training for the ministry. He was engaged to a beautiful girl, soon to be married at our church. What was going on? I was overwhelmed with grief and confusion. I was full of questions and there seemed to be no adequate answers. Where was God in all of this?

This was to be the first of many moments I would spend at the Wall during my lifetime. Quite a few years later, in October of 1990, my mother had a massive heart attack at the Los Angelos airport while waiting to catch a flight to visit my sister in Portland Oregon. She ended up on life support, long enough for us to fly from Australia to see her, but she never regained consciousness and in a few days she was gone. No chance to say goodbye. Her life was cut off in her mid 60s. Our whole family was overwhelmed with grief.

In 2007, my mother-in-law. Renate Myer (affectionally known as Oma, which is German for grandmother), was misdiagnosed with thyroid when in fact she had advanced bowel and stomach cancer. After we heard this shocking news, she passed away within three weeks. Ten days later all three of our teenagers were involved in a serious car accident and spent the first days of the new year in the emergency department of a hospital. Thankfully, they and their friends eventually recovered from their injuries but we were in shock and grief for quite a while.

I could go on, but needless to say, my journey of faith has included suffering and pain, disappointment and loss. Time at the Wall.

The Others

When we read the Bible, it is easy to be caught up in the stories of faith and triumph, as well as the many healings and miracles that took place long ago. But for every hero of faith who had a breakthrough, there were 'others' who didn't see the answer to their prayer. Yet, they also were described as men and women of faith (see Hebrews 11:35-40). In fact, I would suggest that it takes a stronger and deeper faith to continue to trust God in the face of difficulty, suffering and unanswered prayer than it does when everything is going just fine. Let's remember these stories too:

- **Abraham** was promised that he would become a great and large nation, but his wife Sarah spent many long years barren without even one child.
- **Job** was the most righteous person on earth in his day but he suffered terrible tragedies and, although he lived to see better days, he never really found out why.
- **Joseph** was thrown into a pit by his jealous brothers then sold as a slave into Egypt where he spent 13 long years in a prison for crimes he did not commit.
- **Moses** spent 40 long years in the backside of the desert wondering where God was and processing his failed attempt to help his people who were held captive in Egypt.
- The people of **Israel** were excited to be delivered from slavery in Egypt by the power of Yahweh, but going through the wilderness on the way to the promised land was far less enjoyable for them. The deadly hazards of the desert and 'manna' for dinner every day instead of those delicious leeks and garlics back in Egypt was not what they signed up for.
- **David** had to grapple with the consequences of his moral failure of committing adultery with Bathsheba and orchestrating a plot to have her husband killed at war.
- **Elijah** became so depressed after a confrontation with the prophets of Baal that he became suicidal and

God had to help him work through this extreme emotional low.
- **Daniel** was thrown into a lion's den for continuing to pray to his God while in Babylon.
- **Peter** boldly declared that he would never deny Jesus only to do so three times. We are told that he went out and wept bitterly. He was overcome by guilt, shame and regret.
- All of **the disciples** were shocked when Jesus was crucified. Two of them, on the road to Emmaus, said, "We had hoped that he was the one" (Luke 24:21). You can feel the huge disappointment in their words.
- **Paul** spent long years in prison, had ministry friends desert him, was beaten and stoned (with real stones), experienced shipwreck multiple times, and battled with a 'thorn in the flesh' (something obviously very painful) that God never took away from him.

These people all spent time at the Wall. They came to realize that bad things sometimes happen to good people. We all stumble and fall. Life is not all sunshine. There are rainy and even stormy days when we wonder where God is. Hitting a Wall in our journey of faith is not unusual. It is normal. There is nothing wrong with us. We are in good company.

Defining Moments

Our time at the Wall, once referred to by the Spanish mystic and poet St. John of the Cross as 'the dark night of the soul', can become a pivotal or defining moment in our lives. But this is not everyone's story. Our choices about how we respond at this time become crucial.

Some people choose to **deny** that the Wall even exists and, therefore, refuse to engage with it fully. They try to move back to the first three stages of faith and end up staying at a superficial level of faith. However, simply repeating "God is good all the time, all the time God is good" is an inadequate approach to the reality of the Wall.

Other people **defect** on their faith. They give up and walk away. It becomes too hard for them. This is not what they expected. They don't think they can trust a God who allows suffering. For them, either God is powerful and not good or he is good but not powerful. They can't figure it out and so they simply walk away from God and their faith.

Then there are those who seek to **deepen** their faith by surrendering afresh to God in the midst of their questions, doubts, and uncertainty. They do their best to work with God *through* this Wall experience, refusing to respond with the denial that leads to mere superficiality and refusing to defect on their faith in God despite their questions and doubts. After all, doubt can sometimes be the back door to an even stronger faith. This third approach takes great courage. Of course, if we refuse to engage with this stage in our spiritual journey, not only does our own faith not deepen, we become inadequate guides for others who will also inevitably pass this way.

I still don't understand why Robert's life was seemingly cut short at age 20, so full of potential. But for me, it was a 'defining moment'. It was at his funeral that I committed my life fully to following Jesus. I had been somewhat of a 'yo-yo' Christian up until that time. During his memorial service, they read from his personal journal about his deep love and commitment to God. The very next day I started my own journal and dedicated my life fully to God. Though I have wavered at times, I have never looked back from that day.

One day I hope to see Robert again and I will thank him. He lived a short life but his death impacted my life and I will forever be grateful. At a young age, I realized that life is short and frail. We have one chance to live it to the full. Each day, I try to do that.

All around us there is pain and suffering. Every day people somewhere are working through questions of meaning, sickness, loss, the death of a loved one, the failure of a once respected leader, a suicide in the family, depression, divorce, a wayward teenager, tragedy, a natural disaster, an accident, unemployment, bankruptcy, conflict or even war. These are not good things. However, as C.S. Lewis once said, "God often shouts to us in our pain." Yes, sometimes, our pain has a purpose and our mess becomes part of our life message. Not always, but often. At the time we most likely won't see it but one day we may look back and see these experiences as defining moments in our journey of faith.

Can We Do Better Than Job's Friends?

The man Job, as recorded in the Bible, experienced far-reaching and intense suffering. Repeated tragedies struck his livestock, his children, and eventually his own health (Job 1:13-19; 2:7-8). Job's three friends heard about his troubles and came to comfort him. They did well for seven days as they simply sat and cried with him, in complete silence (Job 2:11-13). But when they opened their mouths, they began to theologize and philosophize about 'why' Job was going through this suffering and how he could get out of it quickly. They accused him of being in sin and of not having enough faith. In the end they became his enemies, rather than his friends.

Can we do better than Job's friends? Can we do better when people around us suffer? How easy it is to jump to conclusions, trying to figure out 'why' bad things happen to good people. In the end, we can do a lot of damage and fail to provide the support and empathy that our friends need. When someone is at the Wall, they simply need our presence, a listening ear, and a shoulder to cry on.

Your Story?

I can guarantee, if you have lived long enough, that you too have experienced your own fair share of pain and disappointment. I'm sure there has been some tears. I am certain that you have unanswered questions. You too have spent time at the Wall. Welcome to the journey of faith.

Take a moment to reflect back on your own journey. Do you identify with this stage of faith? What has been your experience? What feelings and emotions do you sense even right now? What have you learnt? What questions do you still have?

Don't rush this. Lean into it. Consider some of the further reading suggestions mentioned on the next page. Then, when you are ready, move on to the next chapter.

For Further Reading

A Grief Observed by C.S. Lewis (HarperOne, San Francisco, CA. 2011).

Breathing Under Water: Spirituality and the Twelve Steps by Richard Rohr (Franciscan Media, Cincinnati, OH. 2011).

Disappointment with God: Three Questions No One Asks Aloud by Phillip Yancey (Zondervan, Grand Rapids, MI. 1997).

Falling Upwards: A Spirituality for the Two Halves of Life by Richard Rohr (Jossey Bass, San Francisco, CA. 2011).

God on Mute: Engaging the Silence of Unanswered Prayer by Pete Greig (Baker Books, Ada, MI. 2012).

The Inward Journey by Gene Edwards (Seedsowers, Jacksonville, FL. 1982).

The Tale of Three Kings: A Study in Brokenness by Gene Edwards (Tyndale House Publishers, Carol Stream, IL. 1992).

Where is God When Its Hurts? by Philip Yancey (Zondervan, Grand Rapids, MI. 2002).

SURRENDER

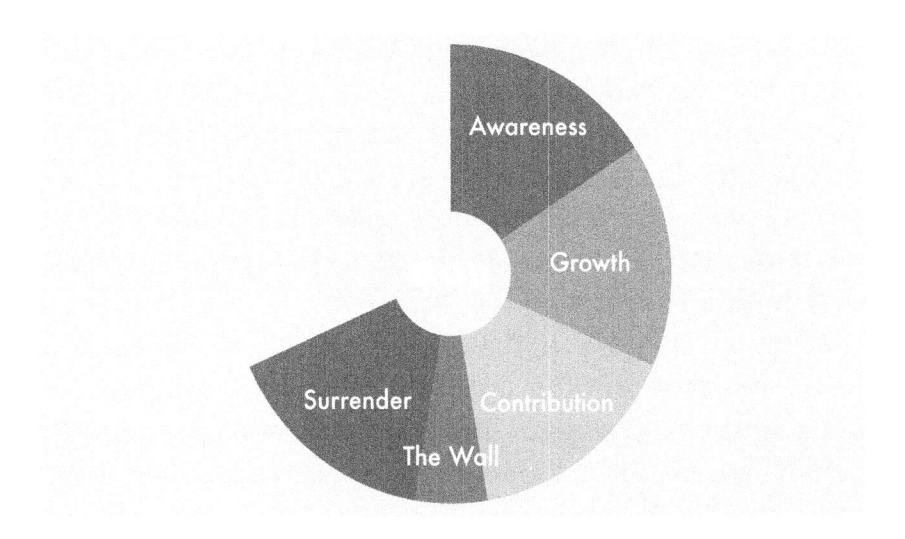

I would like to call the next stage in our spiritual journey **surrender**. Here we embrace the reality that we are not in control and we place our life completely in God's hands. We accept uncertainty. We acknowledge that God's ways are higher than ours.

The Sovereignty of God

This time of fresh surrender is not mere resignation to a limp fatalism. After all, our lives are not subject to luck, fate, or chance. God is sovereign. The **apostle Paul** puts it this way:

> "And we know that God causes everything to work together for the good of those who love God and are called according to his purpose for them." Romans 8:28. NLT

Notice that it does not say, "God causes all things". He does not. There are other forces at work in the world. It also does not say that, "All things are good." They are not. Sickness is not good, nor is an accident, a divorce, or a death. It also does not say, "All things have a happy ending." They don't. Not all students score an 'A' on every test, not all businesses succeed by making a million dollars, and not all marriages last till 'death us do part'. Things don't always turn out as we want them to.

What it does say is that, "God causes all things (the good, the bad and the ugly, the joys and the pains, the bitter and the sweet) to work together for (an ultimate) good because we love God and are called according to his purpose." That's good news.

Joseph spent thirteen long years in a prison, where the power of his dreams were tested. Then in a moment he was promoted to number two next to the Pharaoh in Egypt. Eventually, he came face to face with his brothers who had thrown him into that pit. Overcome with emotion, he made a profound statement:

> "You meant it for evil, but God used it for good." Genesis 50:20.

Joseph did not excuse or minimize what they had done to him. It was wrong, it was hurtful, it was evil. But God used even this harmful act to bring about his purpose in Joseph's life and ultimately in theirs too.

That's a God I can trust, even when I don't understand. This is the God of whom **Job** would say, "Though he slay me, still I will hope in him (Job 13:15)." That's a level of surrender far beyond what takes place in the early stages of our initial awareness of God.

It's the surrender demonstrated by the **three Hebrew children** who when faced with the fiery furnace essentially said, "Our God is *able* to deliver us from the fire and he *will* deliver us from the fire but even *if not,* we will still not bow down to worship other gods" (see Daniel 3:16-18). We all need an "if not" in our faith. This is an incredibly deep level of trust and surrender.

Providence

I once took a class on the providence of God with Graham Cole as part of my Master's of Arts degree in Theology at Ridley College in Melbourne, Australia back in the 1990s. Graham shared with us an illustration from the world of music that shows us some of the different views of how people see the world as functioning.

Some people see the world like a **classical orchestra**. In classical music, individual musicians have little or no freedom. The music has been pre-written by the composer. Everything has been pre-planned - the key and time signature, the exact notes to be played, the tempo and even the phrasing. It's all there, pre-determined. Some people see the world very much like this. God has decided beforehand everything that it is to happen. If something occurs, it must be God's will. We have little freedom or choice. What will be, will be. This is called **determinism**.

Other people go to the other extreme and see the world more like a **jam session**. In a jam session, there is no order or structure. Each musician does his or her own thing. They make a joyful noise. There is no plan. Some people see the world like this. There is no purpose or meaning, so make your own. If it feels good, just do it. This is called **existentialism**.

There is a third option which is a blend and a balance of the previous two. It is called a **jazz band**. With jazz, there is a musical structure but there is freedom within it. There is something called improvisation, where each individual musician decides what they want to play then others respond to that. At times, there is discord or even dissonance but underneath it all, the music is going somewhere. There is structure and chord sequencing as the music continues to move forward. I see the world much like this. We make choices and so do other people. There is freedom and free will. We even make mistakes. But underneath it all, God is at work, carrying the music and the story forward. This is called **providence**.

A Lesson from Cooking

I love to cook. I have a few meals that the family particular love. One of them is a Thai green curry. My wife is an amazing cook too. She has this ability to simply throw things together spontaneously and something amazing usually comes out. Of course, she could never do it exactly the same again. In contrast, I follow the instructions in the recipe book - exactly, but with occasional improvisation.

One of the things I have noticed with my curry recipe is that there are certain ingredients in there that you would not want to eat all by themselves. Who would ever want to drink a glass of fish sauce? Or eat a tablespoon of chilli flakes? These ingredients by themselves are actually unpleasant but it is amazing when you mix everything together what a delicious flavor they create.

Our lives are very much the same. Each of us have had unpleasant and even painful experiences along our journey of faith, but isn't it amazing how God can mix everything together and make something beautiful of our life when we surrender fully to him.

Fresh Surrender

Wherever you are in your spiritual journey, may you come to a fresh surrender in God. Life is not fair but God is good. He can be trusted. Let's surrender to his ways. I'll finish this chapter with some encouragement from the apostle Paul about this kind of surrender to God's good, pleasing and perfect will:

> *"Therefore, I urge you, brothers and sisters, in view of God's mercy, to offer your bodies as a living sacrifice, holy and pleasing to God — this is your true and proper worship. Do not conform to the pattern of this world, but be transformed by the renewing of your mind. Then you will be able to test and approve what God's will is —his good, pleasing and perfect will." Romans 12:1-3.*

PARADOX

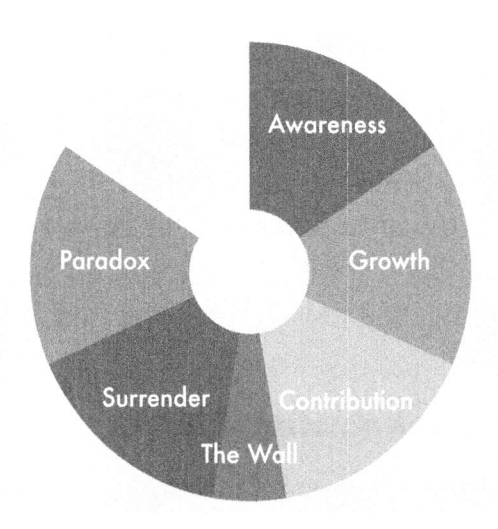

The next stage in our spiritual journey of faith is an embrace of **paradox**. We become comfortable with a new certainty in God while being comfortable with the ambiguity of life. As I mentioned at the end of the last chapter, life is not fair but God is good.

The Now and the Not Yet

Theologically, we live between the 'now' and the 'not yet'.

- Already **sin** has been conquered by Jesus through his atoning work on the cross, but not yet do we sin eradicated from our lives or its affects removed from this world.
- Jesus has conquered **sickness** and disease, but not yet do we see it eliminated from our lives.
- Jesus defeated **Satan**, but not yet is he fully bound and thrown into the lake of fire that he is destined for.

- Jesus triumphed over **death** through his resurrection from the grave, but death remains as the last enemy yet to be fully destroyed.

Welcome to the world of paradox! Here we become familiar with what is referred to as 'liminal spaces'. These are those times when we have let go of one trapeze and we haven't quite yet laid hold on the next one. Talk about uncomfortable! But thankfully there is a net. Underneath are the loving hands of God. But our hearts still feel a little queazy at times.

The Joy of Not Knowing It All

The **apostle Paul** had more revelation and insight than any other human being who has ever lived. He was taken up to the third heaven and saw things too wonderful to speak of (I haven't even been to the first heaven!). He wrote the majority of the New Testament, inspired by the Holy Spirit. Yet listen to these profound words he penned, as recorded in 1 Corinthians 13:12:

> *"Now we see things imperfectly, like puzzling reflections in a mirror, but then we will see everything with perfect clarity. All that I know now is partial and incomplete, but then I will know everything completely, just as God now knows me completely." NLT*

Grasp the wonder of those words. Here is the leading theologian of the Christian faith who met the risen Christ personally and visited the third heaven to receive direct revelation from God. He knows more than most of us will learn about the ways and purposes of God in a lifetime yet he has the courage to say that he does not see things perfectly and that all that he knows is 'partial and incomplete'.

Paul knows he doesn't know it all and he doesn't need to either. I am sure he would have liked to have known everything but he was content to leave the full knowing to God. Here is a faith that is willing to live with mystery ... and one that includes paradox, ambiguity, and even contradictions. Paul doesn't have to figure everything out or control everything in order to believe ... and to fully trust in God.

Here is a man with unbelievable humility. What a contrast to the pride and arrogance that is too common in Christianity today which now has over 39,000 denominations all with their own unique 'statement of faith' believing that they have the complete and right doctrine. And, of course, they are intent on pointing out the heretics among us. How crazy.

This is not a commendation of ignorance nor a denial of the importance of truth. It's a reminder that truth is found in a Person (Jesus) and none of us know it all, which means we need to walk in humility and be willing to learn from each other. It requires that we trust God in areas where we don't understand. That's what faith is all about. There are certain things that reason cannot explain or comprehend.

Ah, the joy of *not* knowing it all ... and not having to. I can rest and put my trust in Christ alone. Paul - may your tribe increase!

Let's be a people who realize we *don't* know it all ... and that's okay. We can still be joyful because we don't have to know it all to walk with this amazing God of grace who we love and serve.

The Mystery of God

Yes, there is a **mystery** to this thing called faith. Everything is not black and white. There is a wonderful rainbow of colors in this God-inhabited universe. God does not fit into our puny boxes. He does not answer all of our questions, just yet. He does not confine himself to our definitions of him nor to our propositions of how he should always act. Jesus himself never healed anyone the same way, yet we so easily want to create formulas for how God always works.

In the words of leading Old Testament scholar Walter Brueggemann, "God is an unsettling God!" To put it another way, as C.S. Lewis' best-selling fiction book *The Chronicles of Narnia* says about Aslan the lion, "No, he is not safe! But he is good." It's time to smash the idols of our safe, small, comfortable, and domesticated god and embrace and accept God for who he is - a God of glory, power, wonder, and mystery.

Welcome to the world of paradox.

LOVE

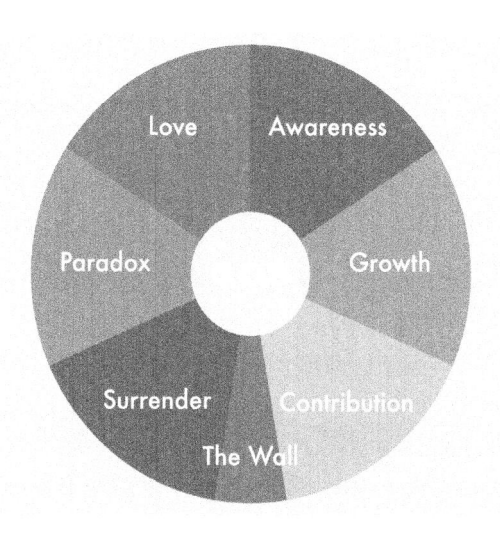

The next stage in our spiritual journey I have simply called **love**. It is here that we give ourselves fully to a life of love - for God and others. We love because God first loved us. We love our neighbor as ourselves.

The apostle Paul elevated love above everything else, including having the gift of prophecy, performing outstanding miracles, and having knowledge of all of God's secret plans - something that he says none of us have anyway (see 1 Corinthians 13). Love, how we treat one another on a daily basis, is far more important than all of these common pursuits for people of faith, demonstrated most profoundly by those who were part of the church in Corinth back in the first century.

A Trinitarian Faith

God is love. He does not just have love nor is he merely a loving person. God *is* love. It is the essence of his nature. The God that Christians worship has revealed himself as one God existing as three persons. A Trinity - Father, Son and Spirit. Not three gods, but one God revealed as three persons living in loving community since before time began. As children of God, we are invited into this dance of love with Divinity.

We normally begin our spiritual journey by coming to know **Jesus**. He is the one who died on the cross to forgive us of our sins. He is our Savior and Lord. We fall in love with Jesus and surrender our lives to him to be his disciples.

But Jesus said he was the way to **the Father**. Through Jesus we become children of God - sons and daughters of the most High God. We come to know that we are loved by the Father.

I knew this in my head for many years while growing up, but it didn't really settle into my heart until I became a dad myself. As I held my firstborn baby son, Josiah, in my arms, I was overwhelmed with love for him. "Take my house or my car or my job but don't take my son", I thought. I then came to realize that my love for him was not based on anything he had done. He had not kicked a goal in a sports game. He had not scored an 'A' on a test at school. He had not made any money yet. In fact, it cost us a lot of money just to get him to this point of his life. He had not *done* anything at all yet I loved him more than anything in this world.

Suddenly, I realized how God the Father feels about me … and you. His love for us is not based on our performance. It is based solely on the fact that we are his children. Once you grasp that kind of love and make it the foundation of your life, you have the capacity to overflow to other people a love like this that is truly unselfish and sacrificial. No wonder Paul prayed in this way in Ephesians 3:14-21:

> *"When I think of all this, I fall to my knees and pray to **the Father**, the Creator of everything in heaven and on earth. I pray that from his glorious, unlimited resources he will empower you with inner strength through his Spirit. Then Christ will make his home in your hearts as you trust in him. Your roots will grow down into **God's love** and keep you strong. And may you have the power to understand, as all God's people should, how wide, how long, how high, and how deep his love is. May you experience the love of Christ, though it is too great to understand fully. Then you will be made complete with all the fullness of life and power that comes from God.*
>
> *Now all glory to God, who is able, through his mighty power at work within us, to accomplish infinitely more than we might ask or think. Glory to him in the church and in Christ Jesus through all generations forever and ever! Amen."* NLT

We then come to know the person of **the Holy Spirit** who has been sent to help us live the Christian life. It is impossible to live the Christian life in our own strength, As

Major Ian Thomas once said, "The Christian life is the life Christ lived back then lived through him now in me."

We are to fellowship with the Holy Spirit. He lives inside of us. You know, it is possible to have someone living in your home with you and never talk to them … though it would be rude. How many Christians never talk to the Holy Spirit, missing out on all of the amazing resources of power, love, and wisdom that he has come to impart to us. Reflect on the following statements:

> "The Friend, **the Holy Spirit** whom the Father will send at my request, will make everything plain to you. He will remind you of all the things I have told you." John 14:6. TMB

> "May the grace of the Lord Jesus Christ, the love of God, and the **fellowship of the Holy Spirit** be with you all." 2 Corinthians 13:14. NLT

> "This is why I remind you to fan into flames the spiritual gift God gave you when I laid my hands on you. For God has not given us a spirit of fear and timidity, but of **power**, **love**, and **self-discipline**." 2 Timothy 1:7. NLT

A Life of Love

At this stage of our faith journey we start to love others more genuinely and deeply than ever before … all based on a revelation of God's love for us. We realize that we are truly loved so we can risk loving others. We die to ego and self and begin to live more for God.

Every year a new word is added to the English dictionary. In 2013, it was the word 'selfie'. Yes, we are a generation obsessed with ourselves, including taking photos of ourselves.

I had a funny but embarrassing experience a year or so back. My wife and I were traveling back to Australia from Sweden where I had spoken at a conference. We had a 24 hour layover in Beijing, China. I had been there before but Nicole had not so we agreed to obtain a short-term airport exit pass, hire a guide, and visit some of the city's amazing sites.

When the day came, we visited the Forbidden City and Tiananmen Square then headed out to see the Great Wall of China. It was an extremely hot day and there were crowds of people everywhere. We arrived at the wall and started the long climb up the thousands of steps to the first tower. It was exhausting, but exhilarating. Nicole started taking photos while I climbed to one of the towers further up. I took a 360 degree panorama video on my iPhone from this magnificent viewpoint.

We then started the long trek back down the hill, into our tour guide's car and back to the airport. Nicole started showing me some of her photos, then I showed her my video. Unbeknown to me, due to the glare of the sun on my phone, I had taken a 360 degree selfie video! Get this. I had just visited one of the great wonders of the world and all I had to show for it was a short video of my ugly, sweaty, sunburnt, unshaven face. How embarrassing!

So what's the point? When our life is over, hopefully it wasn't one long selfie. Let's turn the camera around. Life is not about ME. It's about OTHERS. That's what love is all about.

William Booth, the founder of the Salvation Army, was unable to make a conference he was scheduled to speak at. As an alternative, he sent through a written message with one word on it to be read out to all those who had gathered to be inspired by his speech. "OTHERS", it said. That is what life and ministry is all about.

In their book *The Critical Journey*, Hagberg and Guelich, summarize the life of love by saying, "At this stage we reflect God to others in the world more clearly and consistently than we ever thought possible. We let our light shine in such a way that God is given the credit and the thanks … We have lost ourselves yet truly found ourselves. We are selfless. We are at peace with ourselves, fully conscious of being the person God created us to be. Obedience comes naturally. We give our all without feeling that it means surrender or sacrifice."

Near the End

My beloved dad has travelled the world, written over 60 books and influenced untold thousands of people's lives, including my own. Despite being an orphan with no dad or mum, he did his best to be the dad to my sister and I that he never had.

Right now, at age 91, he is very frail and is living in an aged care home where he has full time care and regular visits from family and close friends. I was sitting with him the other day. I am between two generations. I see myself in my kids and I see myself in my dad. In another three decades or so, I could be where he is. That's a sobering reality. I went home and penned the following poem called "Near the End":

Nearing the end.
Nothing to do.
Just waiting.
In a chair.
Can't read.
Can hardly speak.
Only stare.
Just be there.

Wanting to stay.
Better to go?
It can be confusing.
Near the end.

No more achievements.
No more hills to climb.
No crowds now.
Only family and friends.

Out of the limelight.
Into the shadows.
An unknown face.
In an aged care home.

Life almost over.
What did it all mean?
Did his best.
For God and church.

Notes cast on the waters.
Spread far and wide.

Bread for the hungry.
Seed for the wise.

Followed the call.
Faithful to Him.
Stayed the course.
Finished the race.

Love is all we have.
Near the end.
Love is all we need.
At the end.

I'll finish this chapter by quoting some profound words from Jesus:

> *"Give away your life; you'll find life given back, but not merely given back – given back with bonus and blessing. Giving, not getting, is the way. Generosity begets generosity." Luke 6:38. TMB*

> *"If you grasp and cling to life on your terms, you'll lose it, but if you let that life go, you'll get life on God's terms." Luke 17:33. TMB*

> *"Listen carefully: Unless a grain of wheat is buried in the ground, dead to the world, it is never any more than a grain of wheat. But if it is buried, it sprouts and reproduces itself many times over. In the same way, anyone who holds on to life just as it is destroys that life. But if you let it go, reckless in your love, you'll have it forever, real and eternal." John 12:24-25. TMB*

PUTTING IT ALL TOGETHER

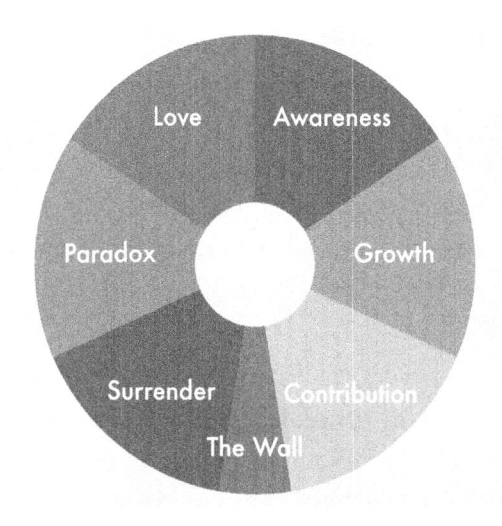

I hope that the **map of the spiritual journey** that I have presented in this book has been helpful to you. The truth is that there is a mystery to our journey of faith. Everyone is unique and will experience variations in their individual journey. I am sure you will agree that it is helpful to view this journey as a circle rather than as a linear progression.

As I said in the opening chapter of this book, this particular map of **the stages of faith** is more *descriptive* than it is *prescriptive*. In other words, it describes the sequence of what *often* happens, not what must or *should* happen. There are many curves, twists and surprises along the way. Sometimes we seem to move in circles, or jump stages, or seem to be in more than one stage at once, or feel stuck, or move in random patterns that don't make sense at the time. No stage is necessarily better than the other.

When we arrive at the stage of **love** we are not finished. We often then move on to a greater awareness of God, further growth and contribution, and inevitably more time at the Wall. Hopefully, we continue to move to deeper and higher levels of faith and experiences with God.

Note that **God** is at the centre. He is present and at work in each stage and our goal is not to try to control our growth experience but to draw closer to him in each season. We are all headed in the same direction – closer to God.

Various stages may be fuzzy and even overlap. We may also re-visit stages at times in no particular order. There are no set formulas for spiritual growth nor can we always know exactly where we are in our spiritual journey. Unfortunately, we also can't control the length of time we may spend in a particular stage or the time we spend transitioning from one stage to another.

The most important thing is that we are more in love with God and we are becoming more like him each and every day. That's the ultimate goal of the spiritual journey.

A Faithful God

The theme of the well-known hymn "Great is Thy Faithfulness" is taken from the book of Lamentations. The prophet Jeremiah wrote this lament during one of the darkest moments of Israel's history. The royal city of Jerusalem had been burned with fire and its people taken away in captivity to Babylon. The entire community of faith was at the Wall.

It was in this very context that Jeremiah penned these timeless, hope-filled words:

"The thought of my suffering and homelessness is bitter beyond words. I will never forget this awful time, as I grieve over my loss. Yet I still dare to hope when I remember this: The faithful love of the LORD never ends! His mercies never cease. **Great is his faithfulness**; *his mercies begin afresh each morning. I say to myself, "The LORD is my inheritance; therefore, I will hope in him!" Lamentations 3:19-24. NLT*

These verses have been a huge encouragement to me during my own times at the Wall. We can say to ourselves, "The LORD is my inheritance; therefore, I will hope in him!" Yes, it is important to talk to yourself. Remind yourself that God is faithful.

As we come to a close, I thought it would be helpful to leave you with some reflection questions. I encourage you to take the time to work through them, by yourself or with a friend or group of fellow pilgrims, as they will help you to embed the concepts and insights we have shared together.

I wish you well on your spiritual journey and leave you with a famous Celtic prayer attributed to St. Patrick:

Christ be with me, Christ within me,
Christ behind me, Christ before me,
Christ beside me, Christ to win me;
Christ to comfort and restore me;
Christ beneath me, Christ above me,
Christ in quiet, Christ in danger,
Christ in hearts of all that love me,
Christ in mouth of friend and stranger.

Reflection Questions

1. Where do you think you are now in your own spiritual journey and why?
2. Where have you been in the past? What stages do you recognize or identify with?
3. Select two biblical characters and see if you can see this pattern in their faith journey.
4. What are some insights for relating well to others who may be at a different stage than you?
5. What sort of activities or experiences might be most helpful at each stage?
6. In what ways can entire families or communities of people experience various stages of faith together (e.g. grief, joy, or awareness of God)?
7. Many churches focus primarily on the first three stages of faith. How can church leaders better equip and prepare followers of Jesus for the full journey of faith will all it nuances and diverse experiences?

RECOMMENDED RESOURCES

Halftime: Changing Your Gameplan from Success to Significance by Bob Buford (HarperCollins Publishing, New York, NY. 2011).

Managing Transitions: Making the Most of Change by William Bridges (Da Capo Lifelong Books, Boston, MA. 2009).

Playing Life's Second Half: A Man's Guide to Turning Success into Significance by David. J. Powell (New Harbinger Publications, Oakland, CA. 2003).

Seasons of the Soul: Stages of Spiritual Development by Bruce Demarest (IVP Books, Downers Grove, IL. 2009).

The Critical Journey: Stages in the Life of Faith by Janet O. Hagberg and Robert Guelich (Sheffield Publishing, Salem, WI. 2005).

The Human Odyssey: Navigating the Twelve Stages of Life by Thomas Armstrong (Sterling Publishers, New York, NK. 2007).

The Land Between: Finding God in Difficult Transitions by Jeff Manion (Zondervan, Grand Rapids, MI. 2010).

The Road Less Travelled: A New Psychology of Love, Traditional Values and Spiritual Growth by M. Scott Peck (Simon and Schuster, New York, NY. 1978).

The Stages of Faith: The Psychology of Human Development and the Quest for Meaning by James W. Fowler (HarperOne Publishers, San Francisco, CA. 1995).

ABOUT MARK CONNER

Mark Conner has been involved in church leadership for over three decades. In February 2017, he transitioned out of the role of Senior Minister at CityLife Church in Melbourne, Australia. Mark is now giving himself to training, writing and coaching others toward greater effectiveness. Mark is a gifted leader, author and speaker who brings a wealth of wisdom and life experience to whatever he engages in. Mark has a genuine love for people and a passion to help them grow and change. He has a Master of Arts degree in Theology from Ridley College in Melbourne, Australia and a Doctor of Ministry degree from Fuller Theological Seminary in the USA. Mark is married to Nicole and they have three adult children.

Visit www.markconner.com.au for more information about Mark's ministry, including details of his speaking schedule and links to videos of his messages.

CONTACT:
Email: mark.conner7@icloud.com
Twitter: @MarkAConner
BLOG: www.blog.markconner.com.au

SUCCESSFUL CHRISTIAN MINISTRY

The Bible teaches that every Christian is a minister. In fact, the church needs more ministers not just more members. Only as every believer discovers their spiritual gifts and begins to serve passionately will we see the church rise up to fulfill its destiny to take the gospel to the nations and be salt and light in each local community. If there ever was a time for every Christian to rise up and take their place in effective ministry, it's right now.

What are the keys to building a high impact long lasting ministry? In this book, Mark Conner shares seven principles for building a successful Christian ministry drawn from his years of ministry experience and observation. Each chapter is packed with practical advice that will empower you to reach your God-given potential and to make a positive difference in the lives of other people.

Available in paperback format from www.word.com.au and in paperback and eBook format from www.amazon.com/author/markconner

PASS THE BATON
SUCCESSFUL LEADERSHIP TRANSITION

There is no success without a successor and Christianity is always one generation away from extinction. These two sobering facts highlight the urgent need for successful leadership transition in today's churches and ministries. CityLife Church (formerly Waverley Christian Fellowship) is a church that has successfully navigated three leadership transitions in its fifty year history. In this informative and practical book, Mark Conner shares vital principles and lessons to help you be more effective with any leadership transition.

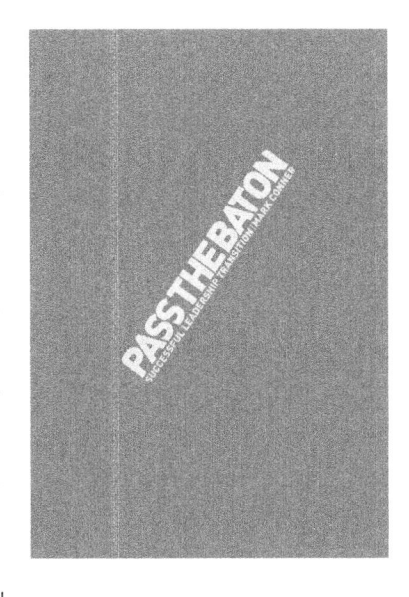

[The Amazon editions include a brief Postscript from 2017 regarding Mark Conner's own transition]

Available in paperback format from www.word.com.au and in paperback and eBook format from www.amazon.com/author/markconner

TRANSFORMING YOUR CHURCH
SEVEN STRATEGIC SHIFTS

If there was ever a need for a healthy, relevant and dynamic churches to emerge, it's right now In today's culture of constant change, how is it possible for a church to remain relevant and effective? In this book, Mark Conner reveals seven strategic shifts that every church must make in order to be effective in the 21st century. These principles will help your church play a vital role in extending the kingdom of God to impact communities, cities and nations for his glory.

"Mark Conner is a superb leader and communicator whose vision has led to remarkable growth in his own church. I am so grateful for his friendship and inspiring example."

Nicky Gumbel Vicar of Holy Trinity Brompton and Developer of ALPHA International

Available in paperback format from www.word.com.au and in paperback and eBook format from www.amazon.com/author/markconner

PRISON BREAK
FINDING PERSONAL FREEDOM

Living in our broken world creates the possibility of becoming trapped by various negative emotions and habits that can easily become like a prison around us. In this helpful book, Mark Conner shares practical principles for finding freedom from common problems such as anger, fear, worry, rejection, depression, addictions, and spiritual bondages. With God's help you can make a prison break - beginning today.

"The book is practical yet sound, both psychologically and biblically and easy to read. I am sure no reader will be disappointed."

Archibald D. Hart. Fuller Theological Seminary

Available in paperback format from www.word.com.au and in paperback and eBook format fromwww.amazon.com/author/markconner

MONEY TALKS
PRINCIPLES FOR FINANCIAL FREEDOM

Australia is one of the richest countries in the world yet, despite this fact, many people are under financial pressure. In this book, Mark Conner shares practical principles for becoming financially free and living wisely with the resources we have. Learn fresh insights about earning, saving, investing, debt reduction and spending wisely. The book also includes extra material on church finances, fundraising and the purpose of business.

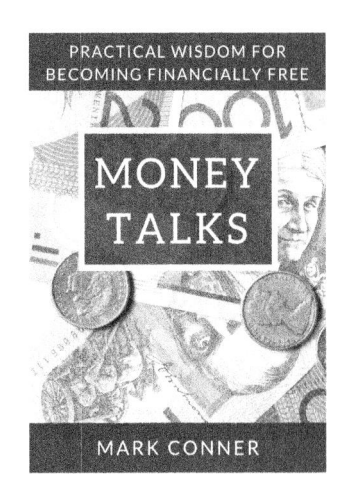

"Countless books on how to use money compete for readers. It is easy to find complicated ones. It is common to find those that just promote getting rich, even by so-called Christians. There are plenty of theoretical studies that are hard to apply and how-to-manuals not based in good theory. But where does one find a short, practical, biblically grounded, clearly written little book that addresses all the important questions about using money in Christian ways with up-to-date charts, graphs and statistics to back everything up? Mark Conner has now written it. Get a copy. Devour it. Then live it out."

Craig L. Blomberg
Distinguished Professor of New Testament. Denver Seminary.

Available in paperback format from www.word.com.au and in paperback and eBook format www.amazon.com/author/markconner

HOW TO AVOID BURNOUT
FIVE HABITS OF HEALTHY LIVING

In a world of rapid change, growing complexity and increasing pressure, stress and burnout are becoming common place. In this practical book, Mark Conner shares five habits for healthy living, gleaned from his decades of experience as an organizational leader and Christian minister.

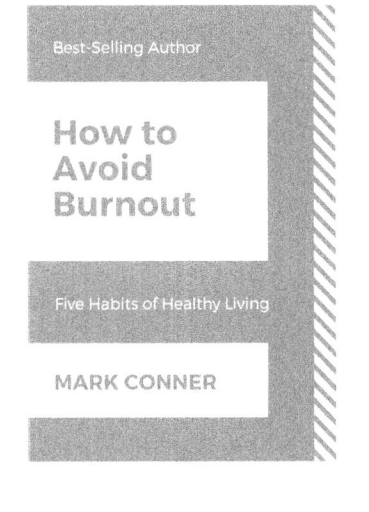

"This book is both timely and important. My 14 years of mentoring a wide range of Christian leaders has convinced me that emotional depletion is widespread and at almost epidemic proportions. If anyone is qualified to write this book it is Mark Conner. He is a long term outstandingly gifted leader with a huge emotional tank who has been very honest about his own journey. The book is well researched and written with very practical guidelines and a rich set of biblical and other references."

Keith Farmer, B.Comm.,B.A.(Hons),D.Min.
Former Principal of Australian College of Ministries

Available in paperback format from www.word.com.au and in paperback and eBook format from www.amazon.com/author/markconner

Printed in Great Britain
by Amazon